CW00821718

FIFTY TWO

NORTHUMBRIAN WALKS

FIFTY TWO

NORTHUMBRIAN WALKS

Written and illustrated by
Ken Bunn

GATESHEAD

METROPOLITAN
BOROUGH COUNCIL
LIBRARIES
AND ARTS

Portcullis Press

First published 1991
This edition published 1996

Portcullis Press and
Gateshead MBC
Libraries and Arts Service
Gateshead Central Library
Prince Consort Road
Gateshead NE8 4LN
Tel : 0191 477 3478
Fax : 0191 477 7454

ISBN 0 901273 29 5

Printed by Chatsworth Studios Ltd.

CONTENTS

EAST

SOUTH

WEST
THE ROMAN WALL

TYNE - WEAR

DURHAM

TEESDALE

INTRODUCTION

There's over six hundred miles in this book and since the opportunity to get out and about doesn't happen every week then there must be enough walks here to keep your feet moving for a few years, through an everchanging landscape of contrasts.. .. from coast to wild moors........by waterfalls and woodland ways........over rolling hills and past peaceful places........to see medieval castles........ to reflect on our Roman Heritage "along the wall" ....and of course to stand on top of Cheviot, Northumbria's highest height.

BOUNDARIES

Any division of Northumbria will be arbitrary There will always be alternatives. The boundaries most acceptable are those that best suit a particular purpose and as accurately as possible outline distinctively different areas. I have chosen divisions which in my opinion are the most relevant for this book.

MAPS

Since no map will ever surpass that of the Ordnance Survey then no walk is really complete without one, using mine as a basic guide. The detail and wealth of information in the Ordnance maps will certainly add to the enjoyment and interest of any walk, as well as helping one not to get lost.

FORMAT

You'll notice an absence of lines and lines of walking directions. There's no need since the Ordnance maps serve perfectly to show the way, and in practice detailed instructions require frequent update.

1

ILLUSTRATIONS
These highlight some of the outstanding visual attractions with the birds and animals being those actually seen "on the day"

TIMINGS
It's perhaps more useful to know approximately how long a walk will take than to be given just the mileage. You can then more accurately plan your own day out. The timings allow for a leisurely pace with one or two short stops of up to fifteen minutes.

RIGHTS OF WAY
The representation of paths and routes in this book should not be taken as evidence of the existence of rights of way.

1996 EDITION
Two walks in this edition are completely new—Ford Circular and Simonside Circular.

KB.

To Northumbrian
country walkers everywhere

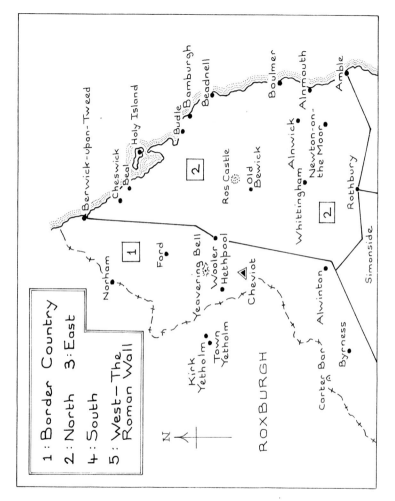

Legend:
1: Border Country
2: North 3: East
4: South
5: West—The Roman Wall

N

Berwick-upon-Tweed
Cheswick
Beal
Holy Island
Budle
Bamburgh
Beadnell
Boulmer
Alnmouth
Amble

Ros Castle
Old Bewick
Whittingham
Alnwick
Newton-on-the-Moor
Rothbury

Norham
Ford
Yeavering Bell
Wooler
Hethpool
Cheviot
Alwinton
Simonside

Kirk Yetholm
Town Yetholm
Carter Bar
Byrness

ROXBURGH

4

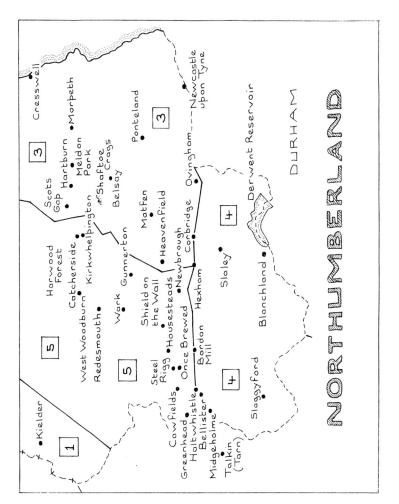

NORTHUMBERLAND

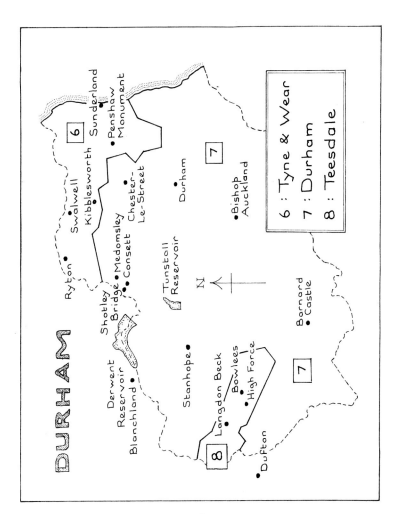

DURHAM

6 : Tyne & Wear
7 : Durham
8 : Teesdale

6

Sunderland
Penshaw Monument
Kibblesworth
Swalwell
Ryton
Medomsley
Chester-Le-Street
Consett
Shotley Bridge
Derwent Reservoir
Blanchland
Tunstall Reservoir
Durham
Bishop Auckland
Stanhope
Langdon Beck
Bowlees
High Force
Dufton
Barnard Castle

N

7

7

8

ORDNANCE SURVEY MAPS
1 : 50 000

1 **BORDER COUNTRY**
   Sheets 74·75·80

2 **NORTH**
   Sheets 75·81

3 **EAST**
   Sheets 81·87·88

4 **SOUTH**
   Sheets 86·87

5 **WEST**
   THE ROMAN WALL
   Sheets 80·81·87

6 **TYNE AND WEAR**
   Sheet 88

7 **DURHAM**
   Sheets 87·88·92·93

8 **TEESDALE**
   Sheets 91·92

ALWINTON CIRCULAR
(KIDLAND FOREST)

Tues 27th Dec.

MAP OS Sheet 80

START	9·05 am
LUNCH	12·35 –
	12·55
FINISH	3·00 pm
DIST	12½ miles app

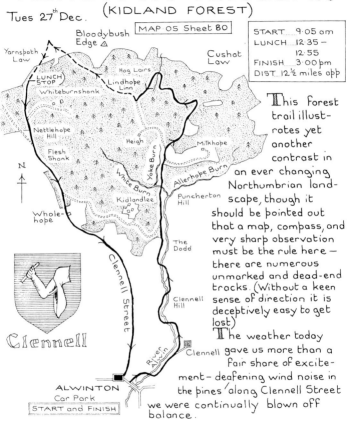

This forest trail illust-rates yet another contrast in an ever changing Northumbrian land-scape, though it should be pointed out that a map, compass, and very sharp observation must be the rule here — there are numerous unmarked and dead-end tracks. (Without a keen sense of direction it is deceptively easy to get lost)

The weather today gave us more than a fair share of excite-ment – deafening wind noise in the pines along Clennell Street we were continually blown off balance.

BERWICK · NORHAM

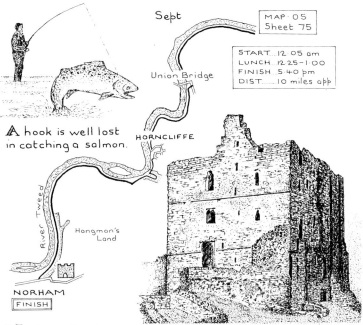

Sept

MAP · 05
Sheet 75

START... 12·05 am
LUNCH... 12·25 – 1·00
FINISH... 5·40 pm
DIST...... 10 miles app

Union Bridge

A hook is well lost
in catching a salmon.

HORNCLIFFE

River Tweed

Hangman's
Land

NORHAM
FINISH

Norham Castle..... known to all who have read Scott's
'Marmion' (...he was a real knight who came here to 'Fame'
the gold-crested helm given him by his lady).

The first wooden motte and bailey castle was set up in
1121; the stone keep (illustrated above) being built around
1160.

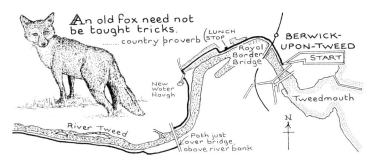

An old fox need not be taught tricks.
........country proverb

LUNCH STOP

BERWICK-UPON-TWEED

START

Royal Border Bridge

New Water Haugh

River Tweed

Tweedmouth

N

Path just over bridge above river bank

This walk allows time to spend the morning in Berwick, which changed hands no less than thirteen times between the old kingdoms of England and Scotland before finally becoming part of the English Crown. Richard the Lionheart ceded Berwick to the Scots in order to finance his crusade........ King John razed the place to the ground.

The Elizabethan town walls are perhaps the finest surviving example of their kind......take a pleasant stroll around the perimeter, or follow the wide path on top of sections of the actual wall.

The Royal Border Bridge, a masterpiece of railway architecture, built by Robert Stephenson between 1847-50 and opened by Queen Victoria.

11

CARTER BAR - BYRNESS

May..... commonly thought to come from
the Roman goddess of growth and increase,
Maia, the mother of Hermes. It has also
been suggested that the name derives
from the Majores or Mairoes, the Senate
of early Rome.

MAP OS Sheet 80

Coquet Head

Chew Green Roman Camp

CARTER BAR
START
Dun Moss
Arks Edge
Leithope Forest
Leap Hill
Fairwood Fell (lunch)
Catcleuch Hill
Hunary Law Hill
Harry's Pike
Forest (pine)
Pennine Way
Ogre Hill
Raven's Knowe
Windy Crag
Houx Hill
Saughy Crag
Byrness Hill

River Rede
A68
Catcleugh Reservoir

N

BYRNESS
church
Inn
FINISH
To Newcastle

START	10·50 am
LUNCH	12·20 – 12·55
FINISH	5·30 pm
DISTANCE	10 miles app

ADDER

This route has the
unique distinction of following the English-
Scottish Border and a stretch of the Pennine Way.

Today we'll never forget — this place was
wetter than wet. Out of the sky came a driving
rain, and over and over again, water and peat
squelched under our feet. Though having said that,
on two brief occasions the sun came out — for
lunch and at the end of the day, for views of the
country array.

CHEVIOT

Jon

HETHPOOL

START and FINISH

College Burn

cottage

N

Whitehall

Southernknowe

MAP OS Sheets 74 (and 80)

START ...... 9·30 am
LUNCH ...... 1·30 - 1·50
FINISH ...... 4·30 pm
DIST .... 14 miles app

Not so much a mountain, more a long flat peat bog (and for most of the year a very soggy peat bog) yet Cheviot is undeniabley the highest place in Northumbria with the approach from the College Valley being an established favourite.

There wasn't a cloud in the sky though the bright weather was bitterly cold with a light covering of snow running along the shaded perimeters of low-lying land. We watched a fox in a frosted field.

From Hethpool a slow pace seemed appropriate with time to appreciate the scenery. The narrow road, superbly sheltered between high hills, becomes a track and reaches a foot-bridge at the valley head, where we stopped for hot drinks before following the burn into the dark and eerie Hen Hole, famed in folklore and legend. It is said there are places here where the sun never enters and even in midsummer it is possible to find a tiny patch of snow.......
...the Snow Egg. Another tradition asserts that a party of huntsmen were led into the Hole by enchanting music and never seen again. There was

13

also Black Adam of Cheviot...... who ravished a bride, robbed the wedding guests, and escaped the bridegroom by leaping into his Hen Hole lair. Today the snow was deep, hard as rock and glass smooth. We proceeded with caution following the tracks of earlier walkers, and chipping other secure holds with our boots. From one exposed high ledge the icicles had crashed down to shatter into hundreds of brilliant fragments reflecting the light of the winter sun. It was as though we were standing on a carpet of diamonds.

Next some physical exertion up to the PENNINE WAY PATH (frozen peat bogs).

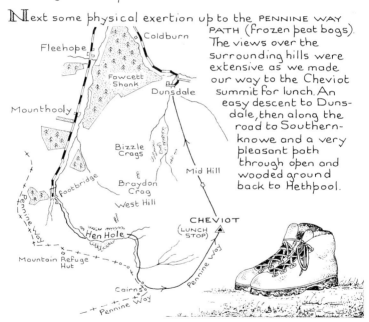

The views over the surrounding hills were extensive as we made our way to the Cheviot summit for lunch. An easy descent to Dunsdale, then along the road to Southernknowe and a very pleasant path through open and wooded around back to Hethpool.

FORD CIRCULAR

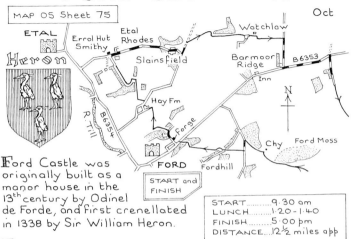

MAP OS Sheet 75

Oct

ETAL

Heron

Errol Hut Smithy

Etal Rhodes

Watchlaw

Slainsfield

Barmoor Ridge

B6353

Inn

N

Hay Fm

R. Till

B6354

Forge

Chy

Ford Moss

FORD

Fordhill

START and FINISH

Ford Castle was
originally built as a
manor house in the
13th century by Odinel
de Forde, and first crenellated
in 1338 by Sir William Heron.

START	9.30 am
LUNCH	1.20 - 1.40
FINISH	5.00 pm
DISTANCE	12½ miles app

Ford village is total
tranquillity... untouched by any sign
of modern intrusion and an ideal
place to start a classic walk of
contrasts. We paused at the forge
and then through woods and fields
up past Hay Farm and on to the
Errol Hut Smithy which makes a
variety of decorative wrought
iron work. At Slainsfield we
wondered what long forgotten battle
or incident had perhaps given this
place its name then trod green roads
and bridleways through open country,
by earth brown ploughed furrows

...the forge

15

Carved rock,
Roughtinglinn

and pastures towards a completely
different landscape of wild moor
before lunch under sheltered pines.
A short road stretch then gently up
and into shaded woods and on to the
carved rock markings at Roughtinglinn
and the very visual evidence of man
in pre-history.... an unexplained
mystery from the period around
3000-1500 BC. From Goats Crag
soon on high ground with the clear
cold air providing perfect weather
conditions for some spectacular distant views. At
Ford Moss an old smelt mill chimney still stands as a
monument to our Industrial Heritage.

About two hours can be
taken off this route by
cutting out the
Doddington Northmoor
section, walking down
the road from
Bar Moor to
Roughtinglinn.

If time permits
visit the old school
before leaving Ford.
Here between 1861 and
1882 Lady Waterford
painted the walls with
a remarkable series of
watercolours illustrating
biblical scenes.

Barmoor
South Moor

Bar Moor

gate

Kembing
Moss

Goats
Crag

Cup and
Ring Marked
Rock

Kembing
Moss Fm

Roughtinglinn

Doddington
Northmoor

Public
Road

B6525 (LUNCH
STOP)

gate

Private Wood

fence

Private Road

KIELDER FOREST

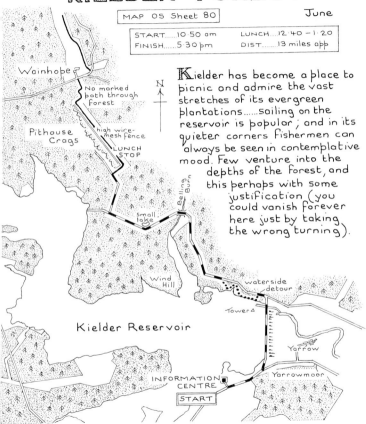

MAP OS Sheet 80

June

START......10·50 am   LUNCH....12·40 - 1·20
FINISH......5·30 pm   DIST.......13 miles app

Kielder has become a place to picnic and admire the vast stretches of its evergreen plantations......sailing on the reservoir is popular; and in its quieter corners fishermen can always be seen in contemplative mood. Few venture into the depths of the forest, and this perhaps with some justification (you could vanish forever here just by taking the wrong turning).

Wainhope

No marked path through forest

Pithouse Crags

high wire-mesh fence

LUNCH STOP

N

Belling Burn

Small lake

Wind Hill

waterside detour

Tower

Kielder Reservoir

Yarrow

Yarrowmoor

INFORMATION CENTRE

START

The waterside detour isn't easy to find or follow If in doubt miss this section and save time.

At the north end of Pithouse Crags turn right, then down the open fire break to Wainhope.

KIELDER CASTLE
FINISH

East Kielder

Ridge End Burn

footbridge (Not shown on OS map)

Hogswood Moor

Three Pikes

the path

Settlement (circular stone enclosure)

Kielder Burn

Greys Pike

Wainhope

The way to the settlement and the Kielder Burn from the wide forest track isn't marked, with the appropriate turn off in the pines being impossible to locate. Judge the distance as best you can on OS map. There is then a well-defined path along the burn and on to Kielder Castle.

WOOLER
WINTER WHITE-OUT

START....11·00 am	FINISH....2·50 pm
LUNCH....12·15–12·45	DIST...5 miles app

MAP OS Sheet 75

Jan

Humbleton

WOOLER

START and FINISH

Woud Ho

Brown's Luw

Wishing Well

Wooler Common (LUNCH STOP)

Earle Whin

Earle

Earlehillhead

N

It was colder than cold, with deep snow on the ground and white flakes falling from the sky. Nevertheless we decided to make a start in the hope that the weather would ease......it didn't. At Wooler Common the farmer allowed us the refuge of his barn for lunch and advised against proceeding further. Wisely we took his advice. Conditions deteriorated rapidly as blinding blizzards made our return route increasingly dangerous.

Back in Wooler the worst weather day so far this winter continued, and over evening dinner at the Tankerville Arms the prospect of being snowed in for the night became a near reality. The sky cleared however, and although a heavy frost set in we were able to get home.

19

YEAVERING BELL

Dec

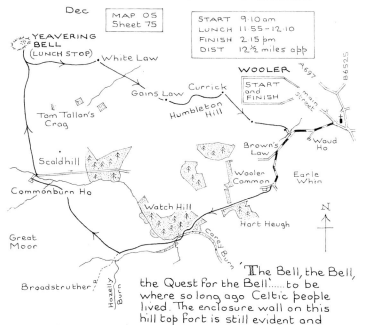

MAP OS
Sheet 75

START   9·10 am
LUNCH   11·55 – 12·10
FINISH   2·15 pm
DIST   12½ miles app

YEAVERING
BELL
(LUNCH STOP)

White Law

WOOLER

START
and
FINISH

A697

B6525

main Street

Gains Law

Currick

Humbleton Hill

Tom Tallon's Crag

Brown's Law

Waud Ho

Scaldhill

Wooler Common

Earle Whin

Commonburn Ho

Watch Hill

Hart Heugh

N

Great Moor

Carey Burn

Broadstruther

Hazelly Burn

'The Bell, the Bell, the Quest for the Bell ..... to be where so long ago Celtic people lived. The enclosure wall on this hill top fort is still evident and surrounds an area large enough to make us realize this was once an important place, with a view commanding a Borderland panorama over fields, hills and plains, castles, villages and battlefields (including the River Glen beside which tradition asserts King Arthur fought).

We walked at a brisk pace today with most of our route being well defined.

20

YETHOLM CIRCULAR

TOWN YETHOLM
START

KIRK YETHOLM
FINISH

July

Pennine Way

Green Humbleton

Halterburn

B6401

Primsidemill

MAP OS Sheet 74

START...10·50 am
LUNCH...12·50 – 1·20
FINISH...5·50 pm
DIST......14 miles app

White Law

Acorn sign.
Pennine Way
'Path
Marker'

For centuries these were debatable lands, violently ruled by feuding factions. Now the only incidents are those inflicted upon lonely walkers by the weather.

Most days you'll meet someone along the last stretch of the Pennine Way, which ends in Kirk Yetholm at the Border Hotel.

Kaim Rig

Settlements

Steer Rig

Black Hag

N

Pennine Way

(LUNCH STOP)

The Schil

Auchope

Birnie Brae

THE COASTAL WAY
ALNMOUTH - BUDLE

Aug

MAP · 05 Sheets 75 and 81

DISTANCE 25 miles app

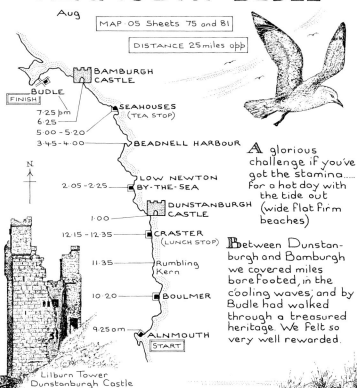

BAMBURGH CASTLE

BUDLE
FINISH

7·25 pm
6·25
5·00 - 5·20
3·45 - 4·00

SEAHOUSES
(TEA STOP)

BEADNELL HARBOUR

LOW NEWTON
BY-THE-SEA

2·05 - 2·25

DUNSTANBURGH
CASTLE

1·00

CRASTER
(LUNCH STOP)

12·15 - 12·35

11·35

Rumbling
Kern

10·20

BOULMER

9·25 am

ALNMOUTH
START

N

Lilburn Tower
Dunstanburgh Castle

A glorious challenge if you've got the stamina..... for a hot day with the tide out (wide flat firm beaches)

Between Dunstan-burgh and Bamburgh we covered miles bare footed, in the cooling waves; and by Budle had walked through a treasured heritage. We felt so very well rewarded.

22

	Sept	Oct
	START	FINISH
BUDLE_____		
BAMBURGH CASTLE____	9·10 am	5·20 pm
SEAHOUSES _____	10·08	3·55 – 4·10
BEADNELL HARBOUR____	11·10 – 11·25	2·27
LOW NEWTON/The BY-THE-SEA/Ship Inn___	12·30 – 1·05 (LUNCH STOP)	12·22 – 1·00 (LUNCH STOP)
DUNSTANBURGH CASTLE_____	1·52	11·20
CRASTER _____	2·13	10·50
RUMBLING KERN____	2·58	10·10
BOULMER _____	3·53	9·15 am
ALNMOUTH _____	5·00 pm	
	FINISH	START
	DISTANCE	DISTANCE
	22½ miles app	19½ miles app

The opportunity arose for two more separate days (different months) walking most of this route, and whilst I usually have a directional preference this turned out to be a classic either way.........
and I can now say at any time of the year.

BEADNELL - BUDLE

Aug

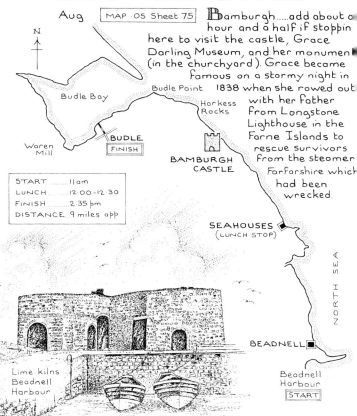

Bamburgh.....add about a hour and a half if stopping here to visit the castle, Grace Darling Museum, and her monument (in the churchyard). Grace became famous on a stormy night in 1838 when she rowed out with her father from Longstone Lighthouse in the Farne Islands to rescue survivors from the steamer Forfarshire which had been wrecked.

Budle Bay

Budle Point

Harkess Rocks

Waren Mill

BUDLE
FINISH

BAMBURGH CASTLE

START 11am
LUNCH ...... 12·00-12·30
FINISH ...... 2·35 pm
DISTANCE 9 miles app

SEAHOUSES
(LUNCH STOP)

NORTH SEA

Lime kilns
Beadnell
Harbour

BEADNELL

Beadnell
Harbour
START

24

The ANGLO SAXON CHRONICLE tells us that Bamburgh was a royal centre by AD 547 when Ida began his reign, though it was his grandson Ethelfrith the Destroyer who gave this place to his wife Bebba, then named Bebbanburgh in her honour.

Nennius, the historian (c.800 AD) who draws on many earlier sources in his writings, suggested that Bamburgh was previously DIN GUAYRDI, which romantic stories (Mallory) recall as the castle given by King Arthur to Sir Galahad; and the Joyous Gard of Lancelot and Guinevere.

The stone castle dates from the Norman Period, and was, due to subsequent centuries of neglect, totally ruinous by the 18th century when Lord Crewe, Bishop of Durham started restoration work. At the end of the 19th century Bamburgh was sold to the first Lord Armstrong who carried out further restoration and reconstruction on an extensive scale.

BAMBURGH CASTLE

BERWICK (TWEEDMOUTH)
BEAL

Jan.

BERWICK-UPON-TWEED
TWEEDMOUTH
START
Spittal
Redshin Cove
Seahouse
N
Cheswick Sands
Goswick
Beal Point
BEAL — Holy Island Causeway
FINISH

START	10.55 am
LUNCH	12.20 - 12.50
FINISH	3.15 pm
WEATHER	Clear, dry, but very cold and windy.
DISTANCE	9 miles app

A quick view of historic border Berwick, then through Tweedmouth harbour and on to the sands keeping continuously as close as possible to the wave-washed shore. During lunch, winter's wet fury lashed down in the distance and cast grey shadows across the sea creating a rainbow (......'that jewelled spectrum from which all colour comes'). Along Cheswick Sands the wind was particularly strong. Near Goswick we paused for about twenty minutes and watched the tide run in over the flats at an alarmingly fast rate.

Our finishing point was the Causeway where the water in a twice daily ritual isolates Holy Island from the mainland. The castle here could be seen in silhouette all day.
........and so away, back to the peopled places of a hurried world.

OYSTER-CATCHER

Holy Island Castle

Scallop
Razor Shell
Cockle
Winkle
Oarweed

26

BOULMER - BEADNELL

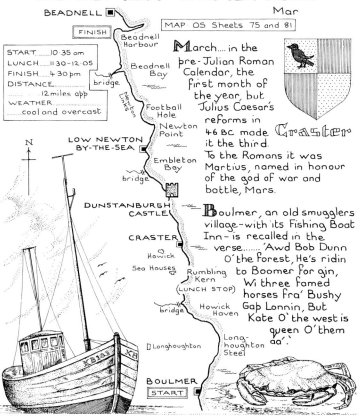

BEADNELL ■

Mar

FINISH

Beadnell Harbour

MAP OS Sheets 75 and 81

START......10·35 am
LUNCH.....11·30-12·05
FINISH.....4·30 pm
DISTANCE.........
..........12 miles app
WEATHER.........
.....cool and overcast

Beadnell Bay

bridge

Newton Links

Football Hole

Newton Point

March.... in the pre-Julian Roman Calendar, the first month of the year, but Julius Caesar's reforms in 46 BC made *Craster* it the third.
To the Romans it was Martius, named in honour of the god of war and battle, Mars.

N

LOW NEWTON BY-THE-SEA ■

Embleton Bay

bridge

DUNSTANBURGH CASTLE

CRASTER

Howick

Sea Houses

Rumbling Kern
(LUNCH STOP)

bridge

Howick Haven

□ Longhoughton

Longhoughton Steel

Boulmer, an old smugglers village – with its Fishing Boat Inn – is recalled in the verse....... 'Awd Bob Dunn O' the forest, He's ridin to Boomer for gin, Wi three famed horses fra' Bushy Gab Lonnin, But Kate O' the west is queen O' them aa'.

BOULMER
START ■

KB109 XH

27

Craster.....the tiny walled harbour seems to evoke the very essence of fishing days and fishing ways, with the village being famous for its cured kippers.

Dunstanburgh Castle.......by a restless and relentless sea stand the remote and impressive ruins of this once great stronghold, where it is still possible to 'touch the history of days gone by.'

We walked northward along a coastline rightly designated an area of Outstanding Natural Beauty.......wide sweeping bays, sand dunes, shell-laden shores, pebbled inlets, amazing twisted rock formations, and grassy paths. Lunch was at Rumbling Kern, the ultimate conception of a real smugglers secret cove (and undoubtedly the landing place of many a contraband cargo). On the beach here we found a marooned squid, and sadly through out the day, many sea birds which seemed to have perished in the recent bad weather.

As always the beaches were deserted, marked only by our boot-prints which the waves erased behind us. Low Newton proved a good place to halt awhile, with the Ship Inn well worth a visit before the last stretch to Beadnell, whose harbour is dominated by a group of perfectly preserved 18th century lime kilns.

DUNSTANBURGH CASTLE

CHESWICK - HOLY ISLAND

June

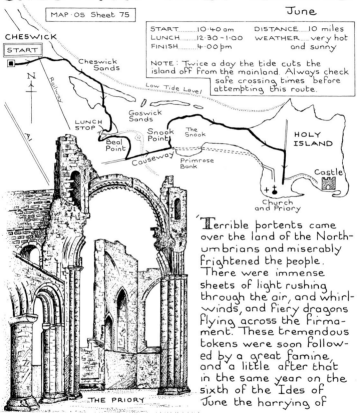

MAP·05 Sheet 75

CHESWICK
START

N

Railway

Cheswick
Sands

Low Tide Level

Goswick
Sands

LUNCH
STOP

Beal
Point

Snook
Point

The
Snook

Causeway

Primrose
Bank

HOLY
ISLAND

Castle

Church
and Priory

START..........10·40 am   DISTANCE.....10 miles
LUNCH..........12·30 – 1·00   WEATHER....very hot
FINISH..........4·00 pm   and sunny

NOTE: Twice a day the tide cuts the
island off from the mainland. Always check
safe crossing times before
attempting this route.

THE PRIORY

Terrible portents came
over the land of the North-
umbrians and miserably
frightened the people.
There were immense
sheets of light rushing
through the air, and whirl-
winds, and fiery dragons
flying across the firma-
ment. These tremendous
tokens were soon follow-
ed by a great famine,
and a little after that
in the same year on the
sixth of the Ides of
June the harrying of

Initial 'M' at the beginning of Saint Mark's Gospel; from the Lindisfarne Gospels created on the island.

THE CASTLE

heathen men miserably destroy-ed God's church in Lindisfarne through rapine and slaughter.

These events were recorded in the 'ANGLO-SAXON CHRONICLE' for the year AD 793 and refer to the coming of the Vikings. Peace and tranquillity now reign to the natural sounds of the birds and the wind, and the continuous ebb and flow of the tide. We trod like pilgrims to pause and reflect in this Cradle of Christianity as once did St. Aidan, Cuthbert, and the Venerable Bede.

On Cheswick Sands we watched the fishermen hauling in their nets. On Holy Island there was a great variety of flowers, though lack of visual birdlife, probably due to the very hot weather.

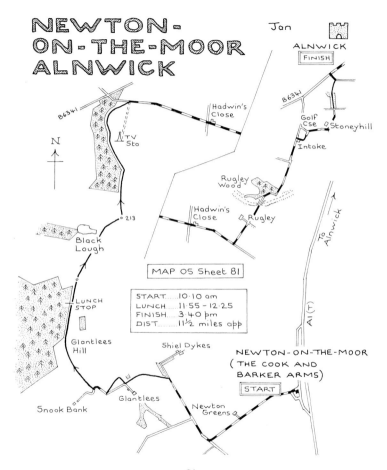

NEWTON-ON-THE-MOOR ALNWICK

Jan

ALNWICK
FINISH

B6341

B6341

Hadwin's
Close

Golf
Cse Stoneyhill

TV
Sta

Intake

Rugley
Wood

Rugley

° 213

Black
Lough

Hadwin's
Close

MAP OS Sheet 81

To Alnwick

A1(T)

LUNCH
STOP

START......10·10 am
LUNCH......11·55 - 12·25
FINISH......3·40 pm
DIST.......11½ miles app

Glantlees
Hill

Shiel Dykes

NEWTON-ON-THE-MOOR
(THE COOK AND
BARKER ARMS)

Snook Bank

Glantlees

Newton
Greens

START

31

ROS CASTLE CIRCULAR
Shown on OS Map as Ross Castle

Jan

MAP 05 Sheet 75

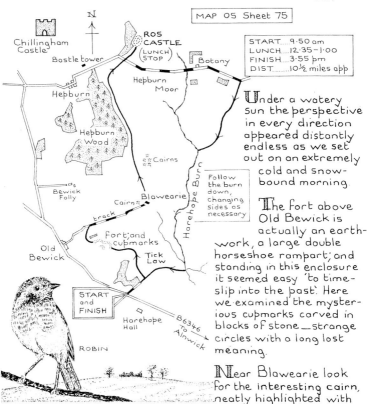

START.... 9·50 am
LUNCH....12·35-1·00
FINISH.... 3·55 pm
DIST...... 10½ miles app

Chillingham Castle

N

ROS CASTLE (LUNCH STOP)

Bastle tower

Botany

Hepburn Moor

Hepburn

Hepburn Wood

Cairns

Follow the burn down, changing sides as necessary

Bewick Folly

Blawearie

Cairn

track

Horehope Burn

Old Bewick

Fort and cupmarks

Tick Law

START and FINISH

Harehope Hall

B6346 To Alnwick

ROBIN

Under a watery sun the perspective in every direction appeared distantly endless as we set out on an extremely cold and snow-bound morning.

The fort above Old Bewick is actually an earth-work, a large double horseshoe rampart; and standing in this enclosure it seemed easy 'to time-slip into the past'. Here we examined the myster-ious cupmarks carved in blocks of stone — strange circles with a long lost meaning.

Near Blawearie look for the interesting cairn, neatly highlighted with

32

stones from the surrounding fields to make it a well maintained monument.

The farm-house at Blawearie is now sadly ruinous, which enhances the isolated romantic solitude of this unique site, with its trees and 'protective' rock formations; so different as to be an island in these rolling hills.

At Ros Castle don't look for any strong tower, the viewpoint is the attraction on this, another double ramparted earthwork fort constructed hundreds of years before the advent of castles as we know them now. Out on the coast, three of Northumbria's real castles ......Lindisfarne Bamburgh and Dunstanburgh stood sharp...... inland, Chillingham Castle and snow-covered Cheviot.

From Ros Castle, a brisk pace (to keep warm) along the road to Botany (rabbits foraging for food) and on to Harehope Burn, secret and unspoilt, where the brown water twists and turns over a succession of rocks, and winds its way through a series of miniature gorges (the haunt of the raven .... we found a nest)

Back near Tick Law, spotted a deer.

WHITTINGHAM ROTHBURY

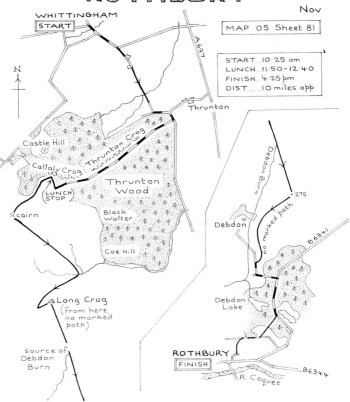

WHITTINGHAM
START

Nov

MAP 05 Sheet 81

START....10.25 am
LUNCH...11.50-12.40
FINISH...4.25 pm
DIST......10 miles app

N

Thrunton

Castle Hill

Thrunton Crag

Callaly Crag

Thrunton Wood

LUNCH STOP

cairn

Black Walter

Coe Hill

Long Crag
(from here, no marked path)

source of Debdon Burn

Debdon Burn

•275

no marked path

Debdon

B6341

Debdon Lake

ROTHBURY
FINISH

B6344

R Coquet

34

AMBLE - CRESSWELL

Jan

AMBLE
START ◯ Coquet Island

N

Druridge Bay

CRESSWELL
FINISH

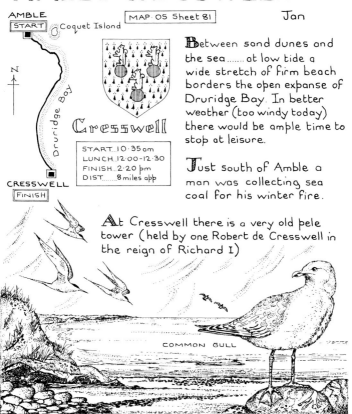

Cresswell

START..10·35 am
LUNCH.12·00-12·30
FINISH..2·20 pm
DIST......8 miles app

Between sand dunes and the sea...... at low tide a wide stretch of firm beach borders the open expanse of Druridge Bay. In better weather (too windy today) there would be ample time to stop at leisure.

Just south of Amble a man was collecting sea coal for his winter fire.

At Cresswell there is a very old pele tower (held by one Robert de Cresswell in the reign of Richard I)

COMMON GULL

35

BELSAY - HARTBURN

Feb

START.....9.55 am
LUNCH......11.50-12.30
FINISH......4.15 pm
DIST.........9½ miles app

Mill Greens
Angerton Station
(LUNCH STOP)
Course of old railway
Angerton Steads
Bolam church
N
Foulmartlaw
How Burn
The Folly
R Blyth
A696 (T)
START
BELSAY

February.....introduced like January into the Roman Calendar by Numa Pompilius. Its name comes from the festival of purification and religious expiation observed during this month, the 'Februa' (latin, februare, to purify).

Bolam Church St Andrew · late Saxon tower...inside a stone effigy of Robert de Reymes, son of Hugh de Reymes of Wherstead, Co Suffolk, acquired the half Barony of Bolam c 1295, built Aydon Castle and Shortflatt Tower which for upwards of three centuries was the home of his descendants....married Maude, daughter of Sir Nicholas de Wortley and grand daughter of Sir William Heron of Ford, took part in all the Scottish wars of that period, and died 1324.

36

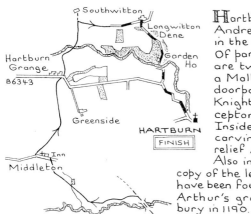

Hartburn Church · St Andrew · consecrated in the early 11th century. Of particular interest are two daggers above a Maltese Cross on the doorpost, indicating a Knights Templar Preceptory here in 1250. Inside, a wooden carving showing in relief Adam and Eve. Also inside is a replica copy of the lead cross said to have been found in 'King' Arthur's grave at Glastonbury in 1190.

Although cold, and windy at times, we walked under a clear blue sky, by hedgerows devoid of leaf and berry, and Hawthorn exposing its black fretwork of branches. In Longwitton Dene saw two deer running for cover......birds seen throughout the day..... Yellow Hammer, Swans (on lake near Hartburn Grange), a Blackbird, Crows, Pheasants and a Robin. The Inn at Middleton proved an ideal afternoon refreshment stop.

Hartburn stands on the line of the mysterious Devil's Causeway – Roman Road.

SWAN

37

BELSAY - PONTELAND

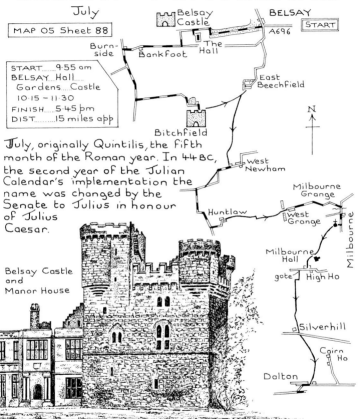

July

Belsay
Castle

BELSAY

A696

START

Burn-
side

Bankfoot

The
Hall

East
Beechfield

START.....9·55 am
BELSAY Hall
 Gardens....Castle
 10·15 — 11·30
FINISH.....5·45 pm
DIST........15 miles app

Bitchfield

July, originally Quintilis, the fifth
month of the Roman year. In 44 BC,
the second year of the Julian
Calendar's implementation the
name was changed by the
Senate to Julius in honour
of Julius
Caesar.

West
Newham

N

Milbourne
Grange

Huntlaw

West
Grange

Milbourne

Milbourne
Hall

gate   High Ho

Belsay Castle
and
Manor House

Silverhill

Cairn
Ho

Dalton

38

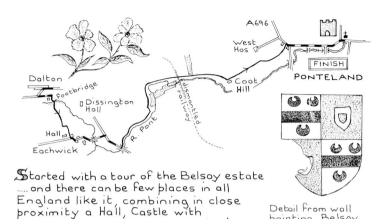

Dalton

Footbridge

Dissington Hall

Hall

Eachwick

R. Pont

dismantled railway

West Hos

A696

Coat Hill

FINISH

PONTELAND

Detail from wall painting, Belsay Castle.

Started with a tour of the Belsay estate ..... and there can be few places in all England like it, combining in close proximity a Hall, Castle with attached Manor House, and a truly unique long Quarry Garden (with an almost unbelievable variety of plants and flowers in sunlit and shaded secret places) I sat alone in a window recess in the castle hall trying to visualize so many hundred years of history now locked away in the silence.

On to Bitchfield with its 15th century tower and 17th century house restored and occupied...... a very impressive country residence.

THE ARMS OF THE

Middletons

OF BELSAY

The track forks south before East Beechfield, and after a short distance...... no marked way. I walked through a fenced wheat field and enclosed pasture to West Newham, and over towards

39

Silverhill through fields as the hay was being cut. To locate the footbridge after Dalton, bear right at the end of the road. The narrow path runs along two sides of a stone garage. Following the River Pont is 'rough going' in places. Near Coat Hill and West Hos, more cultivated fields and fences.

Aylmer

Errington

Ponteland has two ancient structures.......a heavily repaired Vicar's pele tower about which little is known.......and The Blackbird Inn, once the castle of Aylmer de Athol (burnt by the Scots in 1388 as they marched to the Battle of Otterburn), later rebuilt as the manor house of Mark Errington.

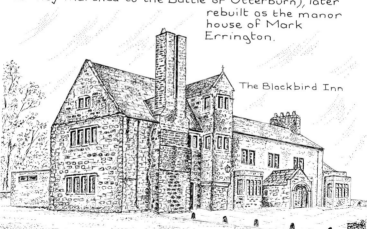

The Blackbird Inn

40

HEAVENFIELD CIRCULAR

Sept

START....10·20 am
LUNCH....12·55–1·15
FINISH....3·20 pm
DIST.......8 miles app

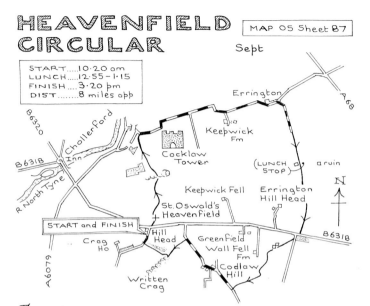

September......when the old Roman year began in March this was the seventh (septem) month, thus September.

There's history on this walk from three very different periods. St. Oswald's stands in splendid isolation and although the only sound heard now at Heavenfield is likely to be from singing in the church or the wild wind, it was here in 635 that the battle cries rang loud as the Christian King Oswald of Northumbria defeated the British King Cadwalla.

From the church gradually down and along the road

41

to Cocklaw Tower, ruinous yet still able to dominate the immediate landscape. From Errington we started to climb gently, by the edge of a ploughed field and through grass pastures, and tucked ourselves behind a dry stone wall for lunch with some fine views to the north. Between the B6318 and Wall Fell Farm, a derelict house of weathered white and grey stone with yellow bales of hay stacked high inside above the open windows. We walked around the perimeter of the adjoining deep green furrowed field speckled with tiny red flowers. Looking back on the perspective of house and field, the visual impact was electric.

Footsteps forward to Written Crag, quarried by the Romans, one of whom left a personal reminder incised in stone.. .. [P]ETRA FLAVI[I] CARANTINI .. .. The rock of Flavius Carantinus. Extensive searching failed to locate the rock (It has been cut out and taken to nearby Chesters Museum).

St. Oswald's, properly called St. Oswald in Lee, the present church dates from 1737.. .. .. of particular interest, a Roman altar.

Cocklaw Tower, probably built in the 15th century by the Erringtons.

42

MATFEN — OVINGHAM

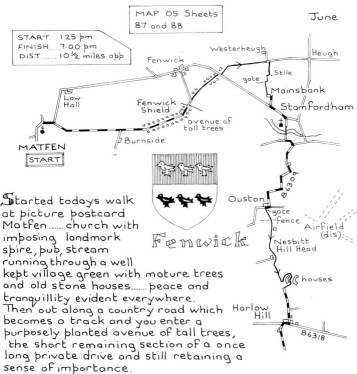

MAP OS Sheets 87 and 88

June

START....1·25 pm
FINISH....7·00 pm
DIST.......10½ miles app

Westerheugh   Heugh

Fenwick

gate   Stile

Mainsbank

Stamfordham

Low Hall

Fenwick Shield

avenue of tall trees

Burnside

MATFEN
START

Fenwick

Ouston

gate
fence

Airfield (dis)

Nesbitt Hill Head

houses

Harlow Hill

B309

B6318

Started todays walk at picture postcard Matfen......church with imposing landmark spire, pub, stream running through a well kept village green with mature trees and old stone houses......peace and tranquillity evident everywhere. Then out along a country road which becomes a track and you enter a purposely planted avenue of tall trees, the short remaining section of a once long private drive and still retaining a sense of importance.

Stamfordham, around its wide village green has all the character of another unspoilt place, with a church

dating back to 1220 and two notable
stone figures ...... a 14th century cross-
legged knight (Fenwick) and the now
legless knight thought to be Sir
John De Felton who in 1390
was Lord of Matfen manor.

Next a road walk, and from
Ouston, over an
unmarked field
path towards
Nesbitt Hill Head,
with a short detour through a
housing estate to pick up the
lane to Harlow Hill and the
road descent to Spital.

The remains of Nafferton Castle can
be seen from the bridge over the A69. It
was never completed, being built without
licence and therefore 'adulterine'. The
ruined keep was later used as the
hide-out of a murderous robber
called Lang Lonkin (hence Lonkins Hall).

Whittle Dene is dense, but with
clearly defined paths. The way through
the woods is in places dark down by
the stream. At Ovingham the
evening sun cast a pale presence
over the Tyne.

bridge

Spital

bridge

Nafferton Castle
(Lonkins Hall) ruin

A69(T)
To Newcastle →

Whittle
Fm

Whittle Dene

N

OVINGHAM
FINISH

River
Tyne

MORPETH (NEWMINSTER ABBEY)
SHAFTOE CRAGS

MAP OS Sheet 81

START..............10·00 am	WEATHER...
LUNCH............12·00-12·35	Cold, clear,
FINISH.............4·05 pm	and windy
DISTANCE........11½ miles app	

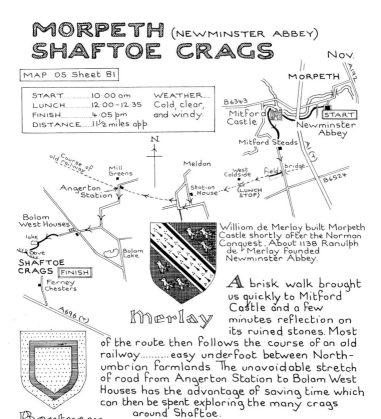

Nov.

MORPETH

N

William de Merlay built Morpeth Castle shortly after the Norman Conquest. About 1138 Ranulph de Merlay founded Newminster Abbey.

A brisk walk brought us quickly to Mitford Castle and a few minutes reflection on its ruined stones. Most of the route then follows the course of an old railway..........easy underfoot between Northumbrian farmlands. The unavoidable stretch of road from Angerton Station to Bolam West Houses has the advantage of saving time which can then be spent exploring the many crags around Shaftoe.

We came off the crags just before darkness fell on this November day.

Bertram
Mitford Castle was built by a Bertram in the reign of Henry II.

Merlay

45

SCOTS GAP
MELDON PARK

Mar

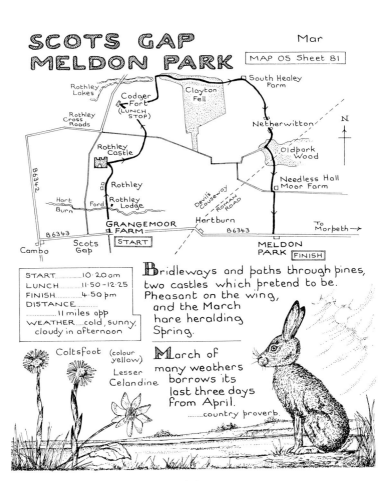

Rothley Lakes

Codger Fort (LUNCH STOP)

Clayton Fell

South Healey Farm

Rothley Cross Roads

Netherwitton

N

Rothley Castle

Oldpark Wood

Rothley

Needless Hall Moor Farm

Hart Burn

Ford

Rothley Lodge

Devils Causeway

ROMAN ROAD

GRANGEMOOR FARM

Hartburn

To Morpeth →

B 6343

Scots Gap

START

B 6343

MELDON PARK FINISH

Cambo

B 6342

START	10·20 am
LUNCH	11·50 - 12·25
FINISH	4·50 pm
DISTANCE	11 miles app
WEATHER	cold, sunny, cloudy in afternoon

Bridleways and paths through pines,
two castles which pretend to be.
Pheasant on the wing,
and the March
hare heralding
Spring.

Coltsfoot (colour yellow)

Lesser Celandine

March of
many weathers
borrows its
last three days
from April.
.......country proverb.

46

BARDON MILL
HALTWHISTLE

MAP OS Sheet 87

Mar

START.....10·15 am
LUNCH...11·40 – 12·10
WAGTAIL HALL
    2·40 – 3·00
FINISH....4·30 pm
DIST......11 miles app

BARDON MILL   START   A69

River South Tyne

footbridge

Beltingham

college

picnic site car park

footbridge

HALTWHISTLE

FINISH

R. South Tyne

Plenmeller

N

R. Allen

LUNCH STOP

Plankey Mill

Kingswood

R. South Tyne

Unthank Hall

Howden Burn

Wagtail Hall

Blackcleugh Rigg

Rock Ho

Kingswood Common

Kingswood Rigg

A thoroughly enjoyable walk with a delightful wooded riverside path up the River Allen before wild open moorland.

In the tiny hamlet of Beltingham..... visit the church.

CORBRIDGE CIRCULAR

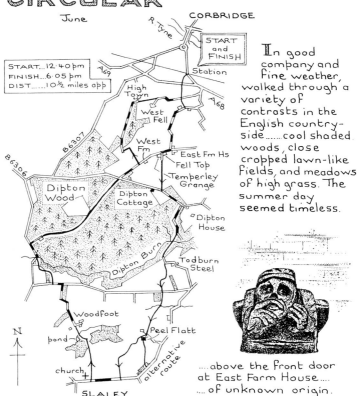

June

MAP 05 Sheet 87

CORBRIDGE

R. Tyne

START and FINISH

Station

START...12·40 pm
FINISH...6·05 pm
DIST......10½ miles app

A69

High Town

A68

West Fell

West Fm

East Fm Hs
Fell Top
Temperley Grange

B6307

B6306

Dipton Wood

Dipton Cottage

Dipton House

Dipton Burn

Todburn Steel

N

Woodfoot

pond

Peel Flatt

alternative route

church

SLALEY

In good company and fine weather, walked through a variety of contrasts in the English country-side......cool shaded woods, close cropped lawn-like fields, and meadows of high grass. The summer day seemed timeless.

....above the front door at East Farm House....
.... of unknown origin.

48

CORBRIDGE-HEXHAM

June

FINISH

MAP OS Sheet 87

B6306

Queen's Cave....... named after
Queen Margaret, wife of Henry
VI, who, with her young son was
given refuge here by a local
robber after her defeat at the
Battle of Hexham in 1464
during the Wars of the

START... 8.30 am
LUNCH (QUEEN'S CAVE)
1.00 - 1.20
FINISH.. 3.00 pm
DIST.... (INCL. CAVE)
13½ miles app

Black
Ho

Queen's
Letch (ruin)

West Dipton Burn
QUEEN'S
CAVE
foot-bridge

Hole Ho

Pub Diptonmill

Roses, and
from where
she was
able to
escape. This
detour from the
foot-bridge should
only be attempted
as an optional
challenge since the
cave is difficult to
locate along
muddy paths
which frequently
cross the burn.
It's approx. 20-
25 minutes up to
a point where a
short wide and
well worn area

Channel
Well

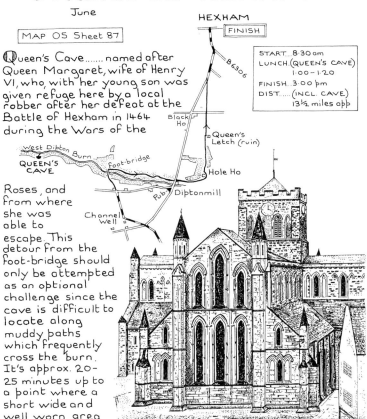

49

slopes up to the narrow entrance (only just visible from the burn). Note also Queen's Letch where tradition recalls her horse stumbled and fell.

The morning started hot in quiet Corbridge. It would have perhaps been more sensible to lie in the sun by the Tyne than walk, though soon in the pine-scented shades of Dipton Wood the path seemed to take control down to the bridge over Devil's Water. Just before the bridge, a meadow of wild flowers surrounded by tree-covered cliffs,

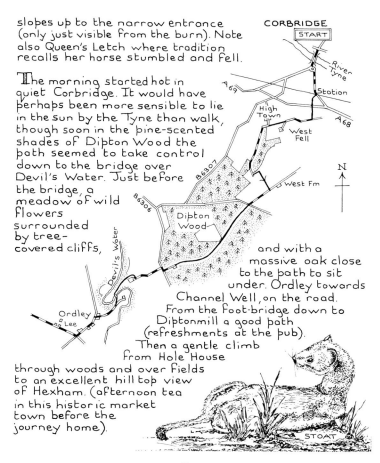

CORBRIDGE
START

River Tyne

Station

A 69

High Town

West Fell

A 68

B 6307

West Fm

N

B 6306

Dipton Wood

Devil's Water

Ordley
Lee

and with a massive oak close to the path to sit under. Ordley towards Channel Well, on the road. From the foot-bridge down to Diptonmill a good path (refreshments at the pub). Then a gentle climb from Hole House through woods and over fields to an excellent hill top view of Hexham. (afternoon tea in this historic market town before the journey home).

STOAT

SLAGGYFORD BELLISTER

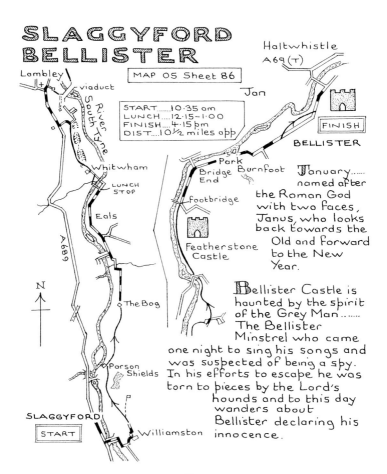

Lombley

viaduct

MAP OS Sheet 86

Haltwhistle
A69 (T)

Jan

FINISH

BELLISTER

START......10·35 am
LUNCH....12·15-1·00
FINISH...4·15 pm
DIST....10½ miles app

River South Tyne

Whitwham

LUNCH STOP

Eals

A689

Park Bridge End

Burnfoot

footbridge

Featherstone Castle

N

The Bog

Parson Shields

P

SLAGGYFORD

START

Williamston

January...... named after the Roman God with two faces, Janus, who looks back towards the Old and forward to the New Year.

Bellister Castle is haunted by the spirit of the Grey Man....... The Bellister Minstrel who came one night to sing his songs and was suspected of being a spy. In his efforts to escape he was torn to pieces by the Lord's hounds and to this day wanders about Bellister declaring his innocence.

51

SLALEY
BLANCHLAND

MAP OS Sheet 87

START....10·15 am
LUNCH....12·15 - 12·50
FINISH...2·45 pm
DIST......8½ miles app

Dec

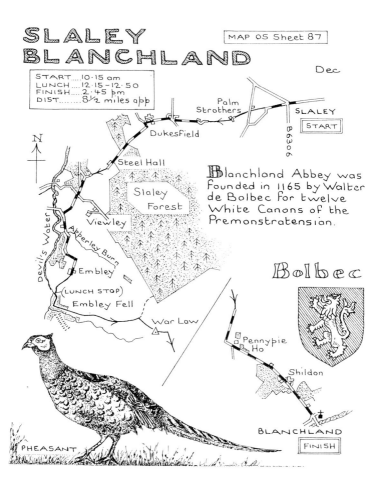

Palm Strothers

SLALEY

START

B6306

Dukesfield

N

Steel Hall

Slaley Forest

Viewley

Abberley Burn

Devil's Water

Embley

(LUNCH STOP)

Embley Fell

War Law

Blanchland Abbey was founded in 1165 by Walter de Bolbec for twelve White Canons of the Premonstratensian.

Bolbec

Pennypie Ho

Shildon

BLANCHLAND

FINISH

PHEASANT

52

TALKIN - MIDGEHOLME

Oct

TALKIN
START

Waygill Hill

START......10·30 am
LUNCH.....12·45 – 1·25
FINISH.....6·20 pm
DIST.........17 miles app

Talkin Head Farm

Talkin △ Fell

Kelky Fell

The Greens

Gairs

Situated between the many attractions of historic Northumbria and the mountains of the Lake District it's not surprising this area remains unspoilt. So few pause long enough to realize that here you can be at one with the elements throughout the hours of a walking day..... in splendid isolation.

We left Talkin village on a sunny autumn morning and were soon on the track beneath Talkin Fell. As always in clear weather we stopped frequently to admire the views. The track reminded me of those old roads of England, once busy and now long forgotten. The land around Gairs seems to have been extensively mined in former times, the house being the obvious centre point of these activities.

On the path above Gairs I noticed on my map the King's Forest of Geltsdale. The

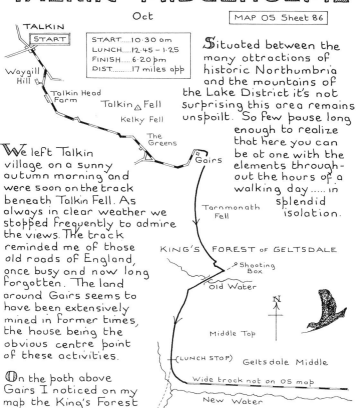

Tarnmonath Fell

KING'S FOREST of GELTSDALE

Shooting Box

Old Water

N

Middle Top

(LUNCH STOP)   Geltsdale Middle

Wide track not on OS map

New Water

53

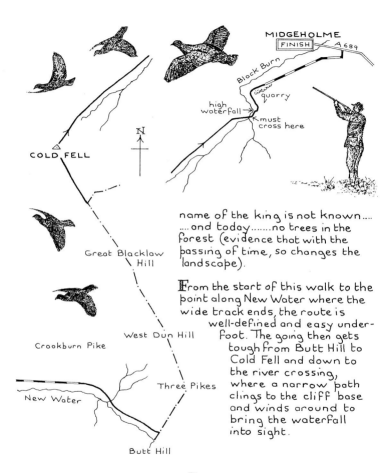

MIDGEHOLME

FINISH   A 689

Black Burn

quarry

high
waterfall →

← must
cross here

COLD FELL

N

Great Blacklaw
Hill

Crookburn Pike

West Dun Hill

Three Pikes

New Water

Butt Hill

name of the king is not known....
.... and today........no trees in the
forest (evidence that with the
passing of time, so changes the
landscape).

From the start of this walk to the
point along New Water where the
wide track ends, the route is
well-defined and easy under-
foot. The going then gets
tough from Butt Hill to
Cold Fell and down to
the river crossing,
where a narrow path
clings to the cliff base
and winds around to
bring the waterfall
into sight.

TALKIN TARN
HALTWHISTLE
Aug

Cleugh Head
(LUNCH STOP)

MAP 05 Sheet 86

START........10·00 am   LUNCH........12·20 – 12·35
FEATHERSTONE........3·15 – 4·30
FINISH........5·45 pm
DISTANCE........14 miles app

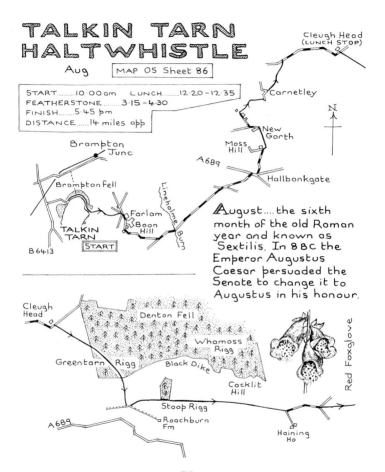

Carnetley

New Garth

Moss Hill

A689

Hallbankgate

Brampton Junc

Brampton fell

Lineholme Burn

TALKIN TARN

Farlam
Boon Hill

START

B6413

August.... the sixth
month of the old Roman
year and known as
Sextilis. In 8 BC the
Emperor Augustus
Caesar persuaded the
Senate to change it to
Augustus in his honour.

Cleugh Head

Denton Fell

Whamoss Rigg

Greentarn Rigg

Black Dike

Cocklit Hill

Stoop Rigg

Roachburn Fm

A689

Haining Ho

Red Foxglove

There is a romantic quality about Featherstone Castle, in its well chosen location and spacious park; and it has its ghosts. Legend relates that a lady of

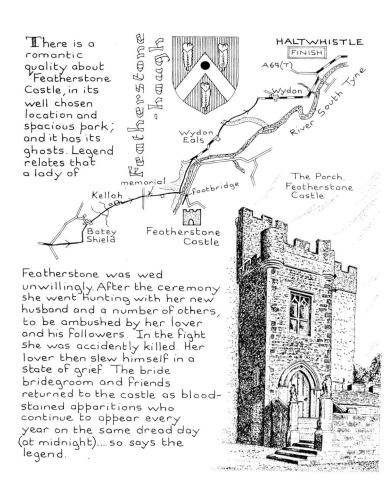

HALTWHISTLE
FINISH

A69(T)

River South Tyne

Wydon

Wydon Eals

memorial

footbridge

Kellah

Batey Shield

Featherstone Castle

The Porch, Featherstone Castle

Featherstone was wed unwillingly. After the ceremony she went hunting with her new husband and a number of others, to be ambushed by her lover and his followers. In the fight she was accidently killed. Her lover then slew himself in a state of grief. The bride bridegroom and friends returned to the castle as blood-stained apparitions who continue to appear every year on the same dread day (at midnight)..... so says the legend.

HARWOOD FOREST ROTHBURY

MAP·05 Sheet 81

April

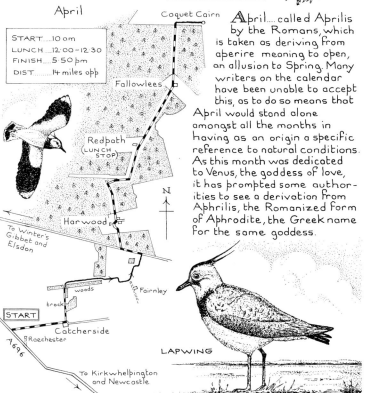

START....10 am
LUNCH....12·00 – 12·30
FINISH....5·50 pm
DIST......14 miles app

Coquet Cairn

Fallowlees

Redpath
(LUNCH STOP)

N

Harwood

To Winter's
Gibbet and
Elsdon

Fairnley

woods
track

START

Catcherside
Raechester

A696

To Kirkwhelpington
and Newcastle

LAPWING

April.... called Aprilis by the Romans, which is taken as deriving from aperire meaning to open, an allusion to Spring. Many writers on the calendar have been unable to accept this, as to do so means that April would stand alone amongst all the months in having as an origin a specific reference to natural conditions. As this month was dedicated to Venus, the goddess of love, it has prompted some authorities to see a derivation from Aphrilis, the Romanized form of Aphrodite, the Greek name for the same goddess.

Along wide tracks and into the forest on a fresh morning,
crisp and cool. Sections of Harwood's 'pine' acres have
recently been felled and re-planted. At Redpath we watched
the Lapwings performing their territorial display flights ....
rising from the ground on a slow beating wing, steadily
climbing...... then into a twisting and rolling dive and rapidly
up again in a flurry of furious
activity, continuously making their
distinctive peewit call. They seem
to repeat these acrobatics until
exhausted.

We took a short rest on Coquet Cairn, then
on through Selby's Cove (a small glacial
canyon named after a local cattle
raider from Coquetdale's
dark past)

ROTHBURY FINISH
R. Coquet

Whitton
Hillhead

Newtown
Park

Simonside   Dove Crag

Simonside   Hills

Weather   Selby's
Head   Cove

The climb onto
Simonside and
Dove Crag was
gentle enough and
both tops are good
places to sit and reflect
at the end of the day.

Coquet Cairn   A cold April and a
full barn.
..... country proverb.

58

HOUSESTEADS ONCE BREWED

July

Steel Rigg
Car Park

Crags

MILECASTLE
39

Crag Lough

Hotbank

Hotbank
Crags

MILECASTLE
37

HOUSESTEADS
Fort
Museum
Information Centre

START or FINISH

N

Peel

MAP · OS Sheet 87

B6318

START.......11·15 am   DISTANCE.......3·7 miles
FINISH........1·45 pm   WEATHER......v. hot · sunny

ONCE BREWED
Information Centre

START or FINISH

'Hadrianus walled this place to stand against the Picts, and here today we walk his Wall as history now befits'.

This section provides spectacular scenery and well preserved stretches of the actual Wall (At milecastle thirty nine it was as though a Legion came, marching through the Mists of Time) We walked at a slow pace, pausing high above Crag Lough to watch the swans and a solitary fisherman; then down into the pine wood and up Hotbank to look back at one of the most photographed views in the area.

At Housesteads as always we visited the recent exhibits and displays from our 'Roman Past'. A popular short walk in either direction.

59

KIRKWHELPINGTON REDESMOUTH

VIA

THE WILDS OF WANNEY

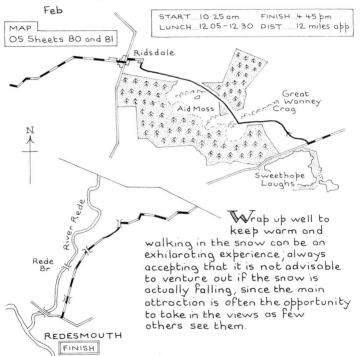

Feb

MAP
OS Sheets 80 and 81

START....10·25 am   FINISH...4·45 pm
LUNCH...12·05 - 12·30   DIST.....12 miles app

Ridsdale

Great Wanney Crag

Aid Moss

Sweethope Loughs

N

River Rede

Rede Br

REDESMOUTH
FINISH

Wrap up well to keep warm and walking in the snow can be an exhilarating experience, always accepting that it is not advisable to venture out if the snow is actually falling, since the main attraction is often the opportunity to take in the views as few others see them.

The road to Plashetts Farm and track over to Sweethope had been levelled to a hard layer of snow.... good under-foot, and although we sat in a blizzard for lunch (crouched up against a stone

KIRKWHELPINGTON

START

Shield o

A696

Three Farms

Lunga Crags

(LUNCH STOP)

Sweethope

Plashetts

forest wall) that proved to be the only squall in a clear day.

We made our way up to Great Wanney Crag.......... everything was white and powder dry. This is the area that originated the north country saying 'in the Wilds of Wanney' and meaning 'in the middle of nowhere'; and whilst the isolation of the place is certainly highlighted in deep mid-winter, a summer visit can be recommended.

KIRKWHELPINGTON
WEST WOODBURN
Feb

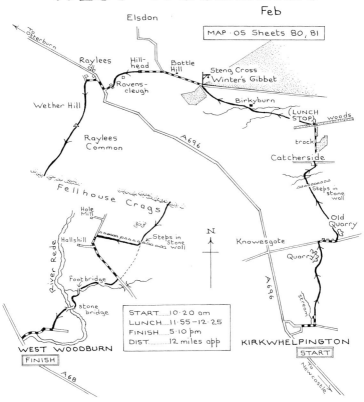

Elsdon

MAP · OS Sheets 80, 81

To Otterburn

Raylees

Hill-head

Battle Hill

Steng Cross
Winter's Gibbet

Ravens-cleugh

Birkyburn

Wether Hill

(LUNCH STOP)

woods

Raylees Common

track

A 696

Catcherside

Fellhouse Crags

Hole Mill

Hallshill

Steps in stone wall

Steps in stone wall

Old Quarry

River Rede

footbridge

N

Knowesgate

Quarry

stone bridge

A 696

stream

WEST WOODBURN

FINISH

START	10·20 am
LUNCH	11·55 – 12·25
FINISH	5·10 pm
DIST	12 miles app

KIRKWHELPINGTON

START

A 68

To Newcastle

Winter's Gibbet · Steng Cross

In 1791 the body of William Winter was hung here in chains, in sight of the place where he had murdered old Margaret Crozier of the Raw, Elsdon. The present Gibbet was erected on the exact site of the original. The large block of stone at the foot of the Gibbet is the base of the Saxon Cross which marked the highest point of this ancient Drove Road, down which cattle were driven from Scotland to the English Market.

A mile further east a group of four trees marks the smithy where the cattle were shod before reaching the metalled roads. Cattle shoes have been found on the site.

-from 'on location' metal plaque-

SKYLARK

NEWBROUGH - WARK

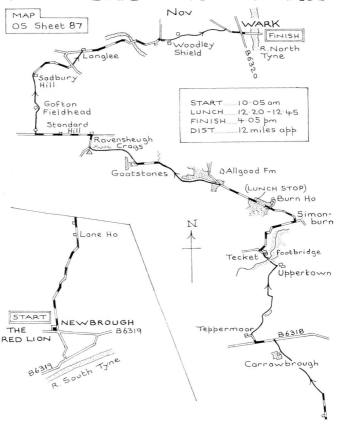

MAP
OS Sheet 87

Nov

WARK
FINISH

Woodley
Shield

R. North
Tyne
B6320

Longlee

Sadbury
Hill

Gofton
Fieldhead

Standard
Hill

START......10·05 am
LUNCH......12·20-12·45
FINISH......4·05 pm
DIST.........12 miles app

Ravensheugh
Crags

Goatstones

Allgood Fm

(LUNCH STOP)
Burn Ho

Simon-
burn

Lane Ho

Tecket   footbridge

Uppertown

START
NEWBROUGH

THE
RED LION   B6319

B6319   R. South Tyne

Teppermoor   B6318

Carrawbrough

N
↑

SHIELD ON THE WALL
GREENHEAD

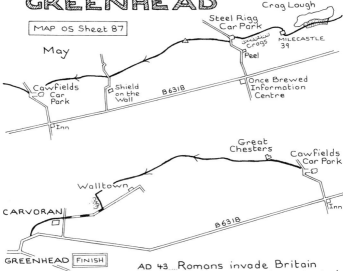

MAP OS Sheet 87

May

Crag Lough

Steel Rigg
Car Park

Peel
Crags

MILECASTLE
39

Cawfields
Car Park

Shield
on the
Wall

B 6318

Once Brewed
Information
Centre

Inn

Great
Chesters

Cawfields
Car Park

Walltown

CARVORAN

Inn

B 6318

GREENHEAD FINISH

AD 43 Romans invade Britain

AD 122 Emperor Hadrian visits Britain........building started
       on the Wall.
" 197 Wall overthrown.......extensive damage
" 211 Wall becomes the effective frontier of Roman
       Britain
" 296 Second attack on Wall
" 300 Rebuilding of the Wall by Constantius Chlorus
" 367 Wall overthrown for third time
" 369 Rebuilding by Count Theodosius....... forts
       became fortified villages
" 383-410 Successive troop withdrawals.

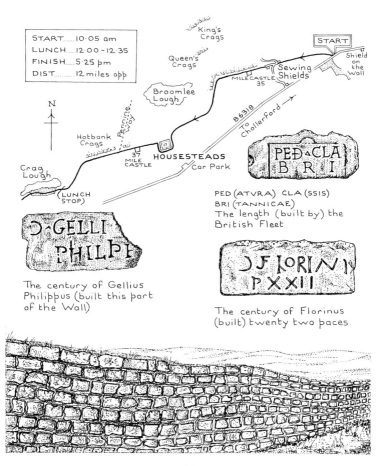

START..... 10·05 am
LUNCH..... 12·00-12·35
FINISH..... 5·25 pm
DIST..... 12 miles app

N

King's Crags

Queen's Crags

START

Shield on the Wall

Sewing Shields

MILECASTLE 35

Broomlee Lough

B6318

To Chollerford

Hotbank Crags

Pennine Way

37 MILE CASTLE

HOUSESTEADS

Car Park

Crag Lough

(LUNCH STOP)

PED·CLA
B R I

PED(ATVRA) CLA(SSIS)
BRI(TANNICAE)
The length (built by) the
British Fleet.

Ↄ GELLI
PHILPPI

The century of Gellius
Philippus (built this part
of the Wall)

Ↄ FLORIN IX
P XXII

The century of Florinus
(built) twenty two paces.

West along the Wall on the most complete 'central sector', with time to visit Housesteads Fort and the Roman Museum at Carvoran.

At Sewingshields, in a field just below the farmhouse, a castle once stood, referred to by Sir Walter Scott in 'Harold the Dauntless' as the Castle of the Seven Shields.

> ....No towers are seen
> On the wild heath, but those that Fancy builds,
> And, save a fosse that tracks the moor with green,
> Is nought remains to tell of what may
>   there have been.

King Arthur..........Legend recalls that long ago in a hall below Sewingshields Castle, King Arthur and his court sat enchanted; to be released only when someone blew a horn that lay on a table near the entrance, and then with 'the sword of the stone' cut the garter placed beside it. None knew where the entrance of the hall was till a local shepherd stumbled upon it. In he went and cut the garter, but forgot to blow the horn. King Arthur was only able to exclaim the following four lines before falling again into the ancient spell.......

> O woe betide that evil day
> On which this witless wight was born,
> Who drew the sword — the garter cut,
> But never blew the bugle-horn.

For the shepherd, fear brought on loss of memory and he was never again able to find the entrance to the hall.

King's Crags and Queen's Crag's are also associated with 'Arthur', who is said to have thrown a twenty ton boulder over a quarter of a mile (some feat) at

Guinevere as she sat combing her hair. (she must have offended him in some way). The queen caught the rock with her comb and it came to rest midway between them, where it now lies, still bearing the marks of the comb.

Arthurian traditions abound in west Northumbria (and Cumbria) and have over the centuries acquired elaboration and distortion, although it becomes evident many are based on lost facts and that the real Arthur (never a king) was in this area in those dark days after the departure of the Romans.

SIMONSIDE CIRCULAR

MAP · OS Sheet 81   Oct   ROTHBURY

START and FINISH

START...10·20 am
LUNCH...12·25-12·45
FINISH...3·20 pm
DIST........
 7½ miles app

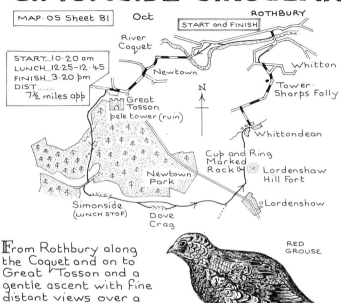

River Coquet

Newtown

Whitton

Tower · Sharps Folly

Great Tosson pele tower (ruin)

Whittondean

N

Cup and Ring Marked Rock

Lordenshaw Hill Fort

Newtown Park

Lordenshaw

Simonside (LUNCH STOP)

Dove Crag

RED GROUSE

From Rothbury along the Coquet and on to Great Tosson and a gentle ascent with fine distant views over a patchwork landscape. The path through the forest is well defined and more interesting than the usual wide tracks. Popular Simonside and Dove Crag are easily climbed. From its size and location the hill fort at Lordenshaw was obviously once an important place. Sharps Folly was built by Thomas Sharp, Rector of Rothbury 1720-1758.

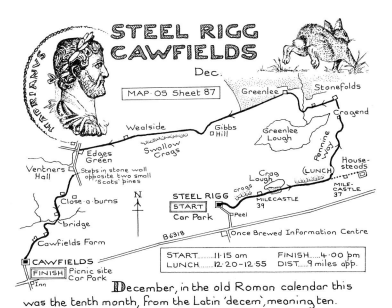

STEEL RIGG CAWFIELDS

Dec.

MAP·OS Sheet 87

START......11·15 am	FINISH......4·00 pm
LUNCH......12·20-12·55	DIST.....9 miles app.

December, in the old Roman calendar this was the tenth month, from the Latin 'decem', meaning ten.

Millions have visited the visible excavations and attractions along the Roman Wall....... thousands have walked the walkable line of its most scenic length; and yet so very few have made the effort to be equally impressed with the sight as seen by the Picts and Scots. Even without a Wall this area has some formidable natural frontiers that only become apparent from the north ; with Winter being the best season to capture the wild and remote atmosphere that seems to be forever present.

WARK-GUNNERTON

Sept

MAP · OS Sheets
80 and 87

START .... 10·15 am
LUNCH .... 12·30 - 1·05
FINISH .... 5·30 pm.
DISTANCE .... 12½ miles app.

Plenty 'country fruits'
at this time of year,
for wine, jam.... Black-
berries, Elderberries,
Haw-berries and Rose
Hips........ also fresh
edible field mushrooms.

Found some Fly
Agaric, a large fungus with
a vivid bright red cap,
spotted white.

Redesmouth
(LUNCH STOP)

dismantled railway

Sheep pens

Buteland

Countesspark Wood

Prestwick Burn

difficult riverside section

Footbridge

Lowshield Green

High Carry Ho

Halywell Burn

Pittland Hills Farm

Thorneyhirst Cottage

dismantled railway

Birtley

Parkhouse Farm

WARK
START

Bridge built in 1878

Chibchase Castle

Short Moor Farm

GUNNERTON
FINISH

River North Tyne

N

SQUIRREL

KIBBLESWORTH SWALWELL

VIA CAUSEY ARCH
THE WORLD'S OLDEST RAILWAY BRIDGE

MAP · OS Sheet 88

Feb

SWALWELL
(THE POACHER)
FINISH

```
START.....9·50 am
LUNCH....11·55 - 12·40
FINISH.....5·10 pm
DIST........14 miles app
```

This walk takes in Beamish Hall — North of England Open Air Museum, which can be visited, time permitting.

Derwent Walk
dismantled railway

To Whickham

Long Hill

N

Sunniside

A692

Marley Hill

Longfield House Fm

dismantled railway

Bobgins Burn

To Tanfield

Causey Arch was built (1725-26) by Ralph Wood, a local mason. It has a 100 feet span, and a deck 80 feet above the stream.

72

THE TANFIELD WAGGONWAY

First waggonway in England	1603	Death of Elizabeth I
	1649	Charles I executed
First colliery at Tanfield recorded	1693	
Causey Arch built	1725-26	
Tanfield colliery burnt out	1740	
	1768	Cook discovers Australia
	1789	French Revolution
	1805	Battle of Trafalgar
	1825	Stockton and Darlington Railway opened
Tanfield waggonway converted to iron rails	1839	
Passengers first carried between Tanfield Lea and Gateshead in horse drawn waggons	1842	
	1854-56	Crimean War
Locomotives replace horses on line	1881	
Tanfield line closed	1962	
Causey Arch restored	1975-81	

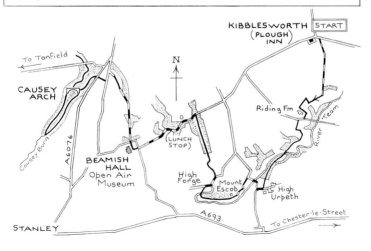

PENSHAW MONUMENT

Mar

MAP · OS · Sheet 88

| START | 9·55 am | LUNCH | 11·55 - 12·35 |
| FINISH | 4·00 pm | DIST | 10 miles app |

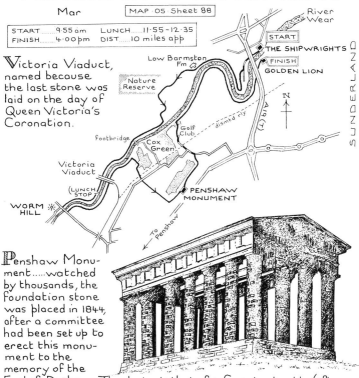

River Wear

START
THE SHIPWRIGHTS
FINISH
GOLDEN LION

SUNDERLAND

Low Barmston Fm

Nature Reserve

A19 (T)

N

dismtd rly

Golf Club

footbridge

Cox Green

Victoria Viaduct

(LUNCH STOP)

WORM HILL

PENSHAW MONUMENT

To Penshaw

Victoria Viaduct, named because the last stone was laid on the day of Queen Victoria's Coronation.

Penshaw Monument.....watched by thousands, the foundation stone was placed in 1844, after a committee had been set up to erect this monument to the memory of the Earl of Durham. The design is that of a Grecian temple (after the temple of Theseus), and it remains today a well known landmark commanding extensive views.

Worm Hill.......Many generations ago, John, heir of the Lambtons, went fishing on a Sunday in the River Wear and caught a worm, which he threw into a nearby well. John grew up and went off to the Crusades in the Holy Land. Meanwhile the tiny worm had grown into a monster, able to wrap itself many times round Worm Hill. It spread terror throughout the area, eating animals and people. John returned to kill the worm as the following ballad describes. Note that the ballad mentions 'Pensher Hill' whereas the actual legend and its association with Worm Hill is of much older origin.

The Lambton Worm

One Sunday mornin' Lambton went
A' fishin' in the Wear;
And catched a fish upon he's heuk
He thowt leuk't varry queer.
But whattn't a kind of fish it was
Young Lambton cuddent tell —
He waddn't fash to carry it hyem,
So he hoyed it in a well!

'Chorus'——
Whisht! lads, haad yor gobs,
An' aa'll tell ye aall an aaful story;
Whisht! lads, haad yor gobs,
An' aa'll tell ye 'boot the worm.

Noo Lambton felt inclined to gaan
An' fight i' foreign wars:
He joined a troop of Knights that cared
For nowther woonds nor scars;
An' off he went to Palistine,
Where queer things him befel,
An' varry seun forgot aboot
The queer worm i' the well.

75

But the worm got fat an'growed
and growed,
An'growed an aaful size ;
He'd greet big teeth, a greet big gob,
An' greet big goggly eyes.
An' when at neets he craaled aboot
Te pick up bits o'news,
If he felt dry upon the road,
He milked a dozen coos.

This feorful worm would of'en feed
On caalves, an' lambs, an' sheep,
An' swally little bairns alive
When they laid doon te sleep.
An' when he'd eaten aal he cud
An' he had hed his fill,
He craaled away an' lapped he's tail
Ten times roond Pensher Hill.

The news ov this myest aaful worm
An' his queor gannins on
Seun crossed the seas, gat te the ears
Of brave an' bould Sor John.
So hyem he came an'catched the beast
An' cut him in twe haalves,
An' thot seun stopped he's eatin' bairns
An'sheep an' lambs, an' caalves.

So now ye knaa hoo aall the foaks
On byeth sides of the Wear
Lost lots o'sheep, an' lots o' sleep
An' leeved in mortal feor.
So let's hev one te brave Sor John
That kept the bairns frae harm,
Saved coos an' caalves by

76

myekin' haalves
O' the famis Lambton worm.

'Chorus'———
Noo, lads, haad yor gobs
Aa've tellt ye aal an aaful story,
Noo, lads, haad yor gobs,
Aa've tellt ye 'boot the worm.

BARNARD CASTLE
CIRCULAR

Nov.

KINGS HEAD HOTEL
......

CHARLES DICKENS STAYED
AT THIS HOTEL ON 2ND FEBRUARY,
1838, WHEN COLLECTING INFORM-
ATION FOR HIS NOVELS
'NICHOLAS NICKLEBY' AND
'MASTER
HUMPHREY'S CLOCK'

Visualize an English
countryside where the
grass is green and rivers
flow close to the stones of
historic places, where in
the autumn gently falling
leaves carpet the woods
like gathered gold, and
there is a timeless peace to
every scene.

Market Hall,
erected 1747.

The weather was mild and clear.
Our lunch stop would be almost
impossible to emulate, where the
waters merge to meet over a
complexity of smooth flat
rocks beneath shaded
trees. Greta Bridge was
sleepy in the sun as we
slowly passed through and
on to St. Mary's Church and
Moor House. The daylight
hours were failing as we
opted for the shorter
route back, viewing
in the distance as
we approached
Barnard Castle
the 'French
palace' Bowes
Museum.

78

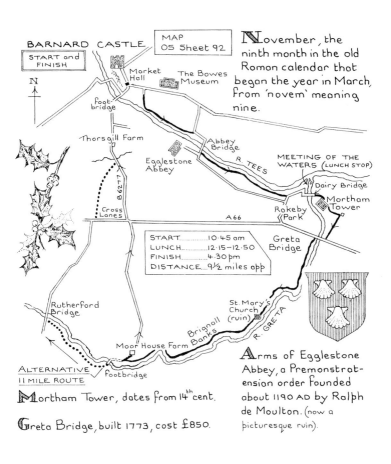

BARNARD CASTLE

START and FINISH

N

MAP
OS Sheet 92

Market Hall

Foot-bridge

The Bowes Museum

Thorsgill Farm

Egglestone Abbey

Abbey Bridge

R. TEES

MEETING OF THE WATERS (LUNCH STOP)

Dairy Bridge

Mortham Tower

Rokeby Park

A66

Greta Bridge

Cross Lanes

B.6277

START............10·45 am
LUNCH..........12·15-12·50
FINISH...........4·30 pm
DISTANCE....9½ miles app

Rutherford Bridge

Moor House Farm

Brignall Banks

St. Mary's Church (ruin)

R. GRETA

footbridge

ALTERNATIVE
11 MILE ROUTE

November, the ninth month in the old Roman calendar that began the year in March, from 'novem' meaning nine.

Mortham Tower, dates from 14th cent.

Greta Bridge, built 1773, cost £850.

Arms of Egglestone Abbey, a Premonstratension order founded about 1190 AD by Ralph de Moulton. (now a picturesque ruin).

79

CHESTER·LE·STREET DURHAM

Aug

MAP·OS Sheet 88

The walk starts 'close to four square Lumley Castle' along what must be a frequently overgrown riverside path. At Lumley Riding look for the track leading south from the front of the house.

Finchale Priory is a surprise to the eyes. The old walls appear almost complete, allowing an informative insight into this religious place founded by St Godric, who came from an adventurous life in Europe (pedlar, seaman, estate bailiff) to Carlisle; and then to Wolsingham where legend relates he had the vision that brought him to Finchale. The year was about 1110 and he was granted permission to establish himself here by Flambard,

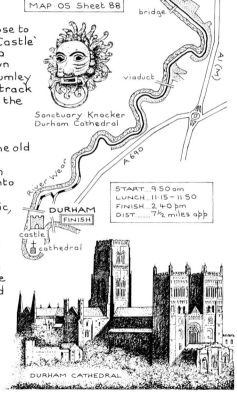

Sanctuary Knocker
Durham Cathedral

bridge

A1 (m)

viaduct

River Wear

A 690

DURHAM
FINISH

castle

cathedral

START....9.50 am
LUNCH...11.15 - 11.50
FINISH...2.40 pm
DIST........7½ miles app

DURHAM CATHEDRAL

80

Bishop of Durham. About a mile upstream from the present priory Godric built his first timber chapel (dedicated to St Mary). Then came the stone structure on the site of the present priory, dedicated to St John the Baptist. It is said that the hermit saint was 105 when he died in 1170.

Around 1237 the plan of the priory was laid out as we see it today, and from the 14th century until its dissolution Finchale was a unique holiday home for the Durham monks. Four monks every three weeks went here for contemplative rest and relaxation.

The stretch from Finchale to Durham is a gem; so close to the ever transient traffic of two major roads, yet in reality so very far removed.

CHESTER-LE-STREET

Lumley Castle

START

B1284

Lumley Riding

A167 (T)

River Wear

N

Great Lumley

A1 (M)

Charles Pit Cottages

FINCHALE PRIORY (LUNCH STOP)

Steps down to footbridge

narrow riverside path

bridge

HERON

CONSETT - STANHOPE

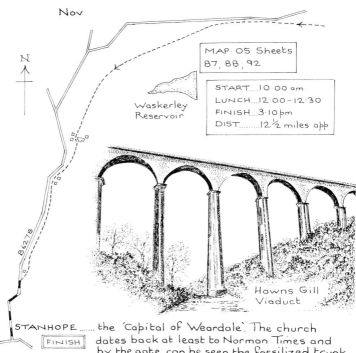

Nov

N ↑

MAP. OS Sheets
87, 88, 92

START....10·00 am
LUNCH...12·00 - 12·30
FINISH...3·10 pm
DIST........12½ miles app

Waskerley
Reservoir

B6278

Howns Gill
Viaduct

STANHOPE ...... the 'Capital of Weardale'. The church
[FINISH] dates back at least to Norman Times and
by the gate can be seen the fossilized trunk
of a tree said to be two hundred and fifty million years
old. The castle was built about 1798 on the site of an
earlier structure. John Wesley the Preacher visited
Stanhope twice in the 18th century.

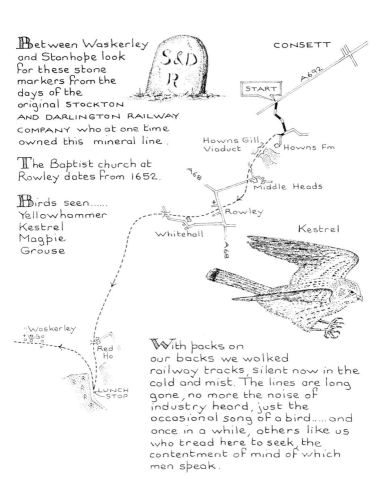

Between Waskerley and Stanhope look for these stone markers from the days of the original STOCKTON AND DARLINGTON RAILWAY COMPANY who at one time owned this mineral line.

The Baptist church at Rowley dates from 1652.

Birds seen......
Yellowhammer
Kestrel
Magpie
Grouse

S&D R

CONSETT

A692

START

Howns Gill Viaduct

Howns Fm

A68

Middle Heads

Rowley

Whitehall

A68

Kestrel

Waskerley

Red Ho

LUNCH STOP

With packs on our backs we walked railway tracks, silent now in the cold and mist. The lines are long gone, no more the noise of industry heard, just the occasional song of a bird..... and once in a while, others like us who tread here to seek the contentment of mind of which men speak.

83

DERWENT SMIDDY SHAW TUNSTALL RESERVOIRS

Mar

MAP OS Sheets
87 and 88

START....10·20 am
LUNCH....12·10 – 12·45
FINISH...5·00 pm
DIST......13½ miles app

Sailing on the
Derwent Res

This is glorious open country through some good stretches of wild moorland and with an easy walking start around to the Derwent Reservoir dam. Under a mid morning sky of rolling cotton wool clouds the weather had a cold edge, though these conditions gave us the views we had hoped for.

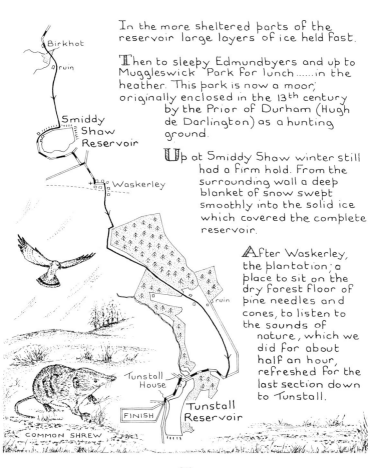

In the more sheltered parts of the reservoir large layers of ice held fast.

Then to sleepy Edmundbyers and up to Muggleswick Park for lunch......in the heather. This park is now a moor; originally enclosed in the 13th century by the Prior of Durham (Hugh de Darlington) as a hunting ground.

Up at Smiddy Shaw winter still had a firm hold. From the surrounding wall a deep blanket of snow swept smoothly into the solid ice which covered the complete reservoir.

After Waskerley, the plantation; a place to sit on the dry forest floor of pine needles and cones, to listen to the sounds of nature, which we did for about half an hour, refreshed for the last section down to Tunstall.

Birkhot

ruin

Smiddy Shaw Reservoir

Waskerley

ruin

Tunstall House

COMMON SHREW

FINISH

Tunstall Reservoir

DURHAM WESTERN HILL
BISHOP AUCKLAND

START.........10·00 am
LUNCH.......12·30 - 1·05
FINISH.......5·00 pm
DIST......14 miles app

Feb

MAP·OS SHEETS
88, 92, 93

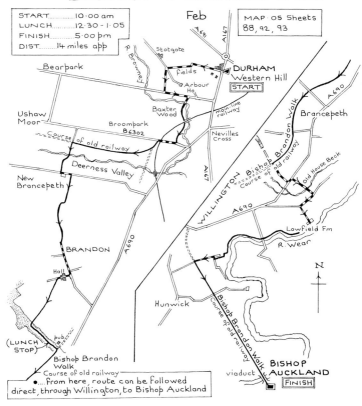

• ... from here, route can be followed direct, through Willington, to Bishop Auckland

86

DURHAM - CONSETT

June

MAP 05 Sheet 88

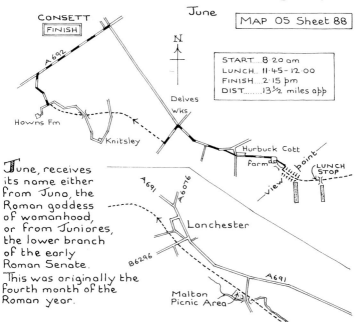

START...8·20 am
LUNCH...11·45 - 12·00
FINISH...2·15 pm
DIST......13½ miles app

CONSETT
FINISH

A 692

Howns Fm

Knitsley

Delves Wks

Hurbuck Cott farm

view point

LUNCH STOP

A 691

A 6076

Lanchester

B 6296

Malton Picnic Area

A 691

June, receives its name either from Juno, the Roman goddess of womanhood, or from Juniores, the lower branch of the early Roman Senate. This was originally the fourth month of the Roman year.

This walk follows for most of the way, the course of the (dismantled) railway which once connected historic Durham City to industrial Consett. It starts along a country lane (in summer bedecked and scented with wild flowers), then over fields to the track above the River Browney and past Stotgate, descending to the bridge just below Bearpark

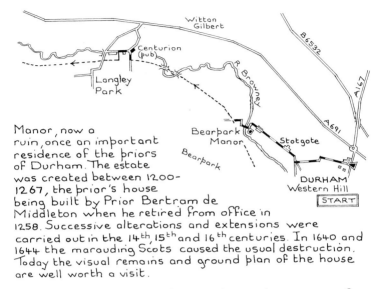

Manor, now a
ruin, once an important
residence of the priors
of Durham. The estate
was created between 1200–
1267, the prior's house
being built by Prior Bertram de
Middleton when he retired from office in
1258. Successive alterations and extensions were
carried out in the 14th, 15th and 16th centuries. In 1640 and
1644 the marauding Scots caused the usual destruction.
Today the visual remains and ground plan of the house
are well worth a visit.

Next, the actual course of the railway through one of
its most scenic stretches to Langley Park and on to
Lanchester, where the outline of the Roman Fort can
still be seen on the hill to the west. Then an amazing
feat of railway engineering (see — view point — on map)
..... a high earth viaduct over the valley. On a fine day
you'll surely stay here awhile, before the road detour
and last section into Consett.

Taking a leisurely pace this route provides plenty of
places perfectly suited for short stops, including the
picnic area at Malton.

MEDOMSLEY · RYTON

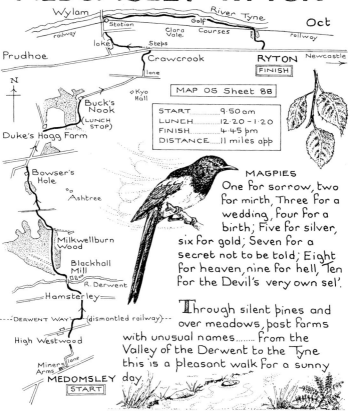

Wylam   River Tyne   Oct

o Station   Clara   Golf
railway   Vale   Courses   railway

loke   Steps

Prudhoe   Crawcrook   **RYTON**   Newcastle

lane   FINISH

N

o Kyo
Hall

MAP OS Sheet 88

START	9·50 am
LUNCH	12·20 - 1·20
FINISH	4·45 pm
DISTANCE	11 miles app

Buck's
Nook

(LUNCH
STOP)

Duke's Hagg Farm

o Bowser's
Hole

o Ashtree

Milkwellburn
Wood

Blackhall
Mill

R. Derwent

Hamsterley

----'DERWENT WAY'-- (dismantled railway)--

High Westwood

Miners' lane
Arms

MEDOMSLEY

START

MAGPIES

One for sorrow, two
for mirth, Three for a
wedding, four for a
birth; Five for silver,
six for gold; Seven for a
secret not to be told; Eight
for heaven, nine for hell, Ten
for the Devil's very own sel'.

Through silent pines and
over meadows, past farms
with unusual names....... from the
Valley of the Derwent to the Tyne
this is a pleasant walk for a sunny
day.

89

SHOTLEY BRIDGE
BLANCHLAND

Oct

MAP OS Sheets 87 and 88

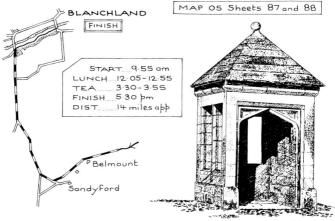

BLANCHLAND

FINISH

START ...9·55 am
LUNCH ...12·05-12·55
TEA ......3·30-3·55
FINISH ...5·30 pm
DIST ......14 miles app

Belmount

Sandyford

...In Blanchland

Now that it is October, don thy woolly smock.

Country Calendar
Lore

College

Lamb Shield

Pedam's
Oak

TEA
STOP

Stoterley
Hill

October, the eighth month in the pre Julian Roman calendar that began the year in March.

The weather was perfect, cool, clear, and dry. From Shotley Bridge (once famous for the swords of German craftsmen who settled here) we experienced a contrasting balance of scenery from woods and riverside to open fields and wild grouse moors. The autumn colours were a wonder to marvel at in a million shades of green and brown.

SHOTLEY BRIDGE
A694
B6310
B6278
START
Shotley Grove
R. Derwent
Consett
A68
Allensford
N
Shield Fm
Derwent Grange
A68
Coal Gate
LUNCH STOP

Our view on approaching Blanchland could have come straight from a picture postcard of rural England.......solid sandstone cottages and an abbey church in a village steeped in history and legend. Part of the old abbey, now the Lord Crewe Arms Hotel, even has its own ghost, Dorothy Forster, heroine of the first Jacobite Rebellion.

HIGH FORCE

Aug

START....2·15 pm
FINISH...7·00 pm
DIST........8½ miles opp

N

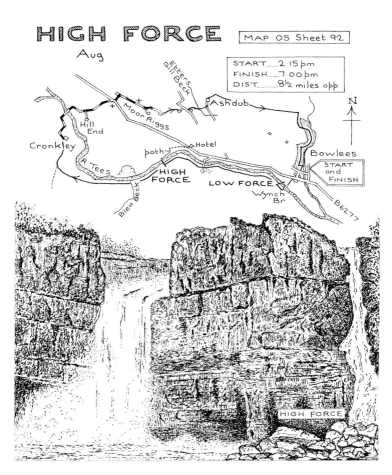

Etters Gill Beck

Ashdub

Moor Riggs

Hill End

Cronkley

R Tees

path

Hotel

HIGH FORCE

Bleo Beck

LOW FORCE

Wynch Br

Bowlees

START and FINISH

B6277

HIGH FORCE

92

High Force is the highest waterfall in the North of England...... stand here and watch the water drop into the dark basin below and you'll be in no doubt. Above the fall, no hint of the spectacular as the River Tees hurries over rock shallows....... downstream and the impressive cataracts of Low Force. Add some wild country (along a section of the Pennine Way), and shaded woods, and this is a well balanced circular walk.

From the start at Bowlees, Wynch Bridge is only minutes away. Close by at Low Force we watched a group of Pennine Way walkers, dipping their bootless feet into the cold water to relieve a few aches and pains. At High Force the expected crowds, though all on the opposite side and unable to cross. Quiet along the path to Cronkley before a series of houses and fields to the woods. If the route finding here proves a little tricky just head for the woods at whatever level. I suspect very few people ever tread these fields; we had to climb over two dry-stone walls where there certainly should have been stiles. In the woods, the most foxgloves I've seen in one place, and in the evening, rabbits.

You may decide just to visit High Force, well worth viewing after heavy rain for maximum visual effect. There's an official path from the hotel.

At Bowlees the chapel has been converted into a Visitor Centre.

Since this is a short walk it provides an opportunity to spend a morning in historic Barnard Castle.

LANGDON BECK-DUFTON

April

MAP·OS Sheet 91

START	11 am
LUNCH	12·20 - 12·45
FINISH	6·00 pm
DIST	13½ miles app

Narrowgate Beacon

DUFTON
FINISH ◇ Stag Inn
Bow Hall   Peeping Hill

Pennine Way   High Cup

Dufton probably derives its name from the Scandinavian 'Dufr' to which was added 'ton', signifying the town or village of Dufr.

High **C**up is a natural amphitheatre of cliffs in a glacial valley whose vast perspective can only be fully appreciated by being there.

The footbridge detour is well worth the effort.....where the stream has cut away a deep narrow gorge in this little known place.

Birkdale

Rasp Hill

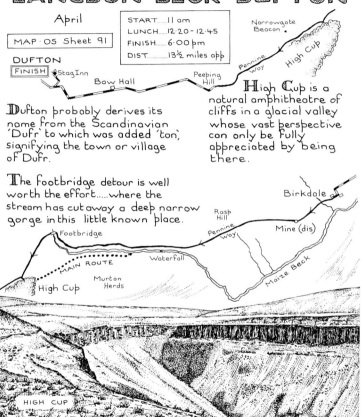

Footbridge

MAIN ROUTE   Waterfall

Pennine Way   Mine (dis)

High Cup   Murton Herds   Maize Beck

HIGH CUP

This is a walk of variations....
pastures, riverbank and rock
scramble, peat fell and moor,
plus two outstanding visual
attractions ...... and at the end
of the day, a walled country
lane.

LANGDON BECK

START

Inn

B 6277

Youth
Hostel

Widdybonk Fell

Widdy
Bank Fm

Pennine
Way

River Tees

Cronkley Scar

Cow Green
Reservoir

N

Holmwath

Cauldron
Snout

Falcon Clints

LUNCH
STOP

Birkdale

Maize Beck

The route takes in
one of the most
interesting sections
of the PENNINE WAY
LONG DISTANCE FOOT-
PATH.

The white water
at Cauldron Snout
cascades over dark
rocks in a perpetual
rush......here we just
stood and admired
the sight of it all before
pushing on along the
track to lonely
Birkdale.

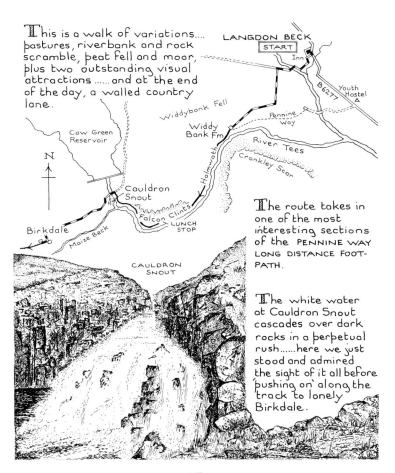

CAULDRON
SNOUT

95

INDEX

A

B

C

J

K

L

INDEX

S

NOTES

NOTES

NOTES

NOTES